YOUR KNOWLEDGE HAS VALUE

- We will publish your bachelor's and master's thesis, essays and papers

- Your own eBook and book - sold worldwide in all relevant shops

- Earn money with each sale

Upload your text at www.GRIN.com and publish for free

Bibliographic information published by the German National Library:

The German National Library lists this publication in the National Bibliography;
detailed bibliographic data are available on the Internet at http://dnb.dnb.de .

Imprint:

Copyright © 2015 GRIN Verlag, Open Publishing GmbH
Print and binding: Books on Demand GmbH, Norderstedt Germany
ISBN: 978-3-668-03674-1

This book at GRIN:

http://www.grin.com/en/e-book/305625/discussion-on-the-ethical-impact-of-the-
internet-on-information-privacy

Victor Kamau

Discussion on the ethical impact of the internet on information privacy

GRIN Publishing

GRIN - Your knowledge has value

Since its foundation in 1998, GRIN has specialized in publishing academic texts by students, college teachers and other academics as e-book and printed book. The website www.grin.com is an ideal platform for presenting term papers, final papers, scientific essays, dissertations and specialist books.

Visit us on the internet:

http://www.grin.com/

http://www.facebook.com/grincom

http://www.twitter.com/grin_com

A Discussion on the Ethical Impact of the Internet on Information Privacy

List of contents

1 Introduction

It is amazing at the rate the internet has roamed our lives. The revolution into our lives has involved advancement in the computer and communications sector. This came with the invention of the radio, telephone and the telegraph. With these advancements there was integration of this compatible capability known as the internet. This is worldwide network coverage with a capability to harness the dissemination of information. It has also facilitated a medium of integrated interactions for computer device users and individuals everywhere in the globe irrespective of the time of access. This experience presents a significant milestone in the sustainable endeavor and commitment to research, production and development. Development in the information sector has been a successful story all through the years since the very fast inventions of electricity. Much effort has also been drawn to the development of this ever dynamic field.

The author tries to identify and analyze the developments that have come along with these tremendous inventions. Much has been focused on the global connectivity by the author targeting the developments in internet use and the consequential impact to the lives of society.

The innovations and developments attached to this entity have occurred in several stages starting from the technological revolution starting with the coming of electricity and the radio. This was followed by advancements in the global approach to research ad operational infrastructure. It is also forms proportion of the social and individual component leading to formations of the famously known as 'internauts' which formed the integral part to communication revolution.

2 Literature Review

The internet now forms the larger proponent of network coverage all over the globe. The information infrastructure has undergone a revolutionary experience that has reached far and wide through the fields of technology and communication and through the entire society and the increased harnessed use of gadgets and equipment usually on the internet.

The very first invention came with the social interactions that have envisioned a worldwide networking and community globalization. The author pays special attention to note that in the evolutionary developments, computers were quickly integrated forming host to host protocol and other networking platforms. The internet was a visionary invention that saw some huge potential in the information sharing through the society's entities as the military, business and the education sectors. Initially the internet was known as the 'ARPANET' which was formally brought online in 1969 having sample trials in several universities in the Southwestern USA (UCLA, Stanford Research Institute, UCSB) leading to other localities all world over.

Such contributions to the formation of the internet were the foundational stones to global social networking and connectivity. As the Internet evolved, one of the major challenges was how to disseminate the deviations to the software, particularly the software that will involve storage of sensitive information concerning individuals, groups, organizations, corporations, institutions and government. The author tries to look back and analyze the approach of incorporating Internet protocols into an integrated operating system for the enquiries and research into the key fundamentals in the positive and widespread adoption of the Internet and the consequential internet safety.

3 Importance of Internet

A key to the speedy progression of the Internet has been the free and sweeping access to the basic documents, social media, research, education encyclopedias and gaming amongst other applications.

3.1 Importance to Society

This invention has been the 'next tool' in the all to do lists of society. This entity has held significant role in the running of the livelihoods. This includes research, development, extension, business and market activities and a social capability to connectivity. Technology is the use of machine or tools that makes things that pretty hard easier to deal with. Technology in communication means the advancement in the electronics like phones and computers. Smart phones are an example of the technology advancement in place. Portable mobile devices have changed the way people live. It has helped then in business transactions and also entertainment. Young people are most inclined to adopt this technology and mot young people love texting a lot.

The older generation is the major user of voice calling services. The middle aged people use the smart phones to transact business. The smart phones and other phones in general as the use of technology has helped in strengthening family and friendship ties. The communication of text messages, calling social networks in smart phones, tablets, laptops and computers at work places has made people get closer emotionally. It is possible to know how the other person is doing without necessarily meeting face to face. We are evolving with internet. Internet has become an integral part of our today lives. Its vast advantages make almost everyone have it. Its connectivity ability makes it a part of our lives and any individual requires it. A person who is used to have connectivity, are occasionally faced with a very hard time when they do not have it.

3.2 Importance to Economy and Business

Of the milestones ever established in the communication sector, the email has had tremendous advances in the economy of nations and the running of business enterprises. It has been a significant factor in all areas of the Internet, and that is definitely true in the growth of protocol stipulations, procedural standards, and Internet operational. Ranging from electronic transfers, banking and business transactions is the major proponents that the internet has contributed to.

3.3 Importance to Media and Information Sharing

Internet is very important as far as popularity is concerned. It drives the fame of a person and makes personality. Media reaches many people at the same time making it very efficient in the propagation. The author also notes talks about a hilarious comedian who earns his fame owing to the media and internet, athletes who make a lot from the internet.

4   Internet Privacy

The most pressing sensation attached to the internet use and its future is the very key factor concerning the privacy of information sharing. As this paper describes the concern of the safety of information that will usually be used in business, economic, military, education and governmental endeavors.

Philosophers and ethicists have termed confidentiality as obligatory distinctive aspect of personal freedom. Confidentiality is related with autonomy, dignity, devoutness, reliance, and freedom. References to the value of sequestered life may be bring into being in the bible, the antiquity of Periclean Athens, as well as the antiquity and culture of many people around the world. The essence of privacy comes a long when one has to do with the consequences of not engaging privacy. Though not a fundamental right, it is essential to withhold in all ways possible to enhance high measures of privacy.

5 Internet Ethics

Numerous strategies have been put in place to enhance safety on the internet. Much effort has been engaged by institutions, government and higher learning entities to help curb this menace of network insecurity. Always good information will need good decisions in handling, sharing and dissemination. Safeguard of information on the internet is essential in avoiding misuse, malicious handling leading to misunderstanding in the society.

The insensitive use and handling of information on the internet may cause serious distress, embarrassment and great disorder. Most lately social media through internet information distortions and disseminations frolicked major roles in the "Arab Spring" unrests in the Middle East, instigating Egypt and Libya to shut down the Internet in their republics in an endeavor to stifle dissension. [18] In China there it has remained an unending battle stuck between the government and activist groups over government watching and expurgation of the Internet.

Insensitive management of critical information on the internet has brought much disparity in the running of governments and normal calamity of governance. In regard to this ethical management is a key component to getting information safeguarded on the internet. Privacy shield is indispensable to precaution against such misuses.

5.1 Importance of Internet Ethics

Most internet providers have ethics that they follow. These ethics aids in the running of the operations. These ethics includes accountability, fairness, integrity, responsibility, professionalism, truth, honesty, maturity, discipline transparency, information assurance among others. Each of these ethics brings an advantage either to the service provider, the employees, stakeholders or the internet users. These ethics impact differently on the usage and information dissemination through the internet.

5.2 Information Safety Assurance

Internet providers as Search engines, e.g. Google, Yahoo, Bing etc. in collaboration with pay – internet subscription providers assure the internet users that the information that they transact through the internet are highly safeguarded from malicious handling. They offer safety to the information passed through the net. This is a sign of upholding ethical management.. It is a moral obligation to ensure that the users get the information that is up to standards. It is ethical to assure the users that the efforts towards safety are fundamental to offering internet safety to users, service for a long time.

5.3 Impact of Internet Ethics on Privacy

The internet ethics used by providers and users has impacted positively on the privacy. This has helped on the reduction of risks due to indiscriminate access to vital, private and sensitive information on the internet. This has also indicated positive returns to the efforts to minimize information violations. Openness has been a special significant result from personal and organizational data protection.

6 Implications to Internet Information Insecurity

Insensitive use of information on the internet conflicting privacy as the author describes all through this paper defines them as matters of concern for the various reasons as discussed herein. The further y profound information is strewn, the greater the jeopardy of booboo, misunderstanding, percipience, preconception and other an ethical uses. Lack of measures to uphold privacy hinder interpersonal, organizational development inhibiting the freedom of thought and the felling attached to ones countenance. This distortions cause an affront to the dignity of oneself while facilitating straining relations amongst the society. In larger extent this may lead to susceptibility of individuals to power of large institutions and those from government.

7 Challenges to Upholding Internet Privacy

The challenge that faces the internet privacy and ethical handling of information includes such aspects as having advances to new technology coming up in the most ever dynamic situations ever. In a broader view advancements may be very useful but having such inventions-to the unethical perception of drilling private and insensitive data from the internet is far from being advantageous.

In the bid to uphold this entity, internet providers end up serving straining efforts in the uphold of ethical handling of information being formal or informal information. Some of the services such as password requests when making access to private and sensitive sites have been mulled by illegal accessibility through the internet where malicious users hack and malpractices on the site.

Being apparent about intricate processes is explicably puzzling for Big Data dealings and the privacy pros fully engrossed in the weeds. The author also notes that folks talk about fostering consumer trust through corporate culpability.

Good companies will be as apparent as possible, but must continuously exhibit to their clients that they are dependable. Clearness is but one step toward a justly accountable society and it's a development that never indeed ends. Efforts to create awareness to users so as to help in the continuous fight of internet malpractice have contributed positively though unsatisfactorily.

8 Recommendations

There is no single entity in the world that is perfect. Every invention and undertaking has its flaws and strongholds. Good recommendation increases the continuity of the endeavors and makes the running of such uphold of privacy easy. Ethics in internet use are prone to changes due to the different situations the information and communication. Sector faces. The author would recommend to a users' approach and the code of conducts to enhance the ethics in internet use.

9 Conclusion

The society needs information comprising personal info, to relate, transact business, economic activity and even in education, research and development. This aids institutions to administrate meritoriously and to protect the haven of their staff, students, clients and citizens in case of government. But users also prerequisite safeguard from the feverish or malicious custom use of that information.

This paper discusses about the ethics in internet use and its impacts to the day to day undertakings in the society. It also discusses the challenges that arise from the implementation of this internet ethics. These challenges affecting the running and regular information dissemination are brought out clearly. This research opens up the mind of the reader to understand the internet ethics in general and their impacts in social order. It is more real because it uses support samples that exist with real statistics. It is evident that the appropriate internet use has a great impact in the way this order is upheld.

References

Andrejevic, Mark 2010 "Cybernetic TV" in FlowTV, volume 7.09, available online at http://flowtv.org/?p=1202 (accessed on 03/28/2013

Birkerts, S. (1994) 'Into the Electronic Millennium' in his The Gutenberg Elegies, New York, Fawcett Columbine, p. 117-133 available at http://archives.obs-us.com/obs/english/books/nn/bdbirk.htm (accessed on 03/28/2012).

L. Roberts, "Multiple Computer Networks and Inter-computer Communication", ACM Gatlinburg Conf., October 1967.

Mark Poster, 'Everyday (Virtual) Life'. Chapter 40, NMTR (full text available at https://muse.jhu.edu/login?auth=0&type=summary&url=/journals/new_literary_history/v033/33.4poster.html (accessed on 03/28/2013).

R. Kahn, Communications Principles for Operating Systems. Internal BBN memorandum, Jan. 1972.

Strianese m (n.d) [online]Code of ethics and business conduct available at http://www.l-3com.com/images/stories/code-of-ethics/english/english.pdf (accessed on 06/05/2013).

YOUR KNOWLEDGE HAS VALUE

- We will publish your bachelor's and master's thesis, essays and papers

- Your own eBook and book - sold worldwide in all relevant shops

- Earn money with each sale

Upload your text at www.GRIN.com
and publish for free